Civil Asset Forfeiture Reform in Texas
Fighting Contraband While Upholding Civil Liberties

Including contributions from

Derek Cohen

Center for Effective Justice, The Texas Public Policy Foundation

Representative David Simpson

Texas House of Representatives

Andrew Kloster

The Heritage Foundation

Shannon Edmonds

Texas District and County Attorneys Association

Matt Miller

Institute for Justice, Texas

Center for Effective Justice
TEXAS PUBLIC POLICY FOUNDATION
900 Congress Avenue | Suite 400
Austin, TX 78701

1

Civil Asset Forfeiture Reform in Texas:
Fighting Contraband While Upholding Civil Liberties is published
in the United States by Right on Crime,
a project of the Texas Public Policy Foundation
in partnership with the American Conservative
Union Foundation and the Justice Fellowship.

TEXAS PUBLIC POLICY FOUNDATION
900 Congress Avenue, Suite 400 | Austin, TX 78701
For more information, please see rightoncrime.com

Book prepared for publication by David Reaboi

Contents

Introduction

Dianna Muldrow
Texas Public Policy Foundation

In early December 2014, the Center for Effective Justice at the Texas Public Policy Foundation had a Civil Asset Forfeiture Primer at the Capitol, where they assembled a panel of policy makers, legislators, and authorities to give their expert opinions on the matter and to take questions from the audience. Andrew Kloster, a legal fellow from the Heritage Foundation that focuses on civil rights issues was present, along with Matt Miller from the Institute of Justice where he fights for property rights. They were joined by Shannon Edmonds from the Texas District and County Attorneys Association and Texas State Representative David Simpson. The Center for Effective Justice's Derek Cohen moderated.

Mr. Cohen began by giving the audience background into the issue of civil asset forfeiture. He mentioned that the idea goes as far back as the Roman Empire and has continued on through out the ages before becoming a bone of contention between England and its colonies before and during the American Revolution. He summed up the issue currently in the terms that it has been referred to by media from all sides. Some look at civil asset forfeiture as an "indispensable tool" for law enforcement and prosecutors while others see it as "policing for profit" and "a sustained assault on the Fifth Amendment and due process."

The speakers eagerly discussed the topic. Andrew Kloster began by delving deeper into the reasoning behind the creation of civil asset forfeiture in the American system and how that has devolved today into an abused mechanism in modern day law enforcement. Shannon Edmonds also chimed in clarifying that civil asset forfeiture was intended to make sure that the proceeds of crime didn't end right back in the pockets of criminals.

But all agreed that the current situation has resulted in spectacular abuses. Families threatened with the removal of their children, owners of small businesses losing their assets, and case after case of small funds and property taken bit by bit from innocent and often helpless citizens. The money is usually enough to make it worth taking, but not enough to justify the legal expense involved in getting it back, leaving most people without representation or due process.

Both Kloster and Miller spoke of the incentive structures that are present in the current system. When law enforcement is making decisions about whether or not they seize assets, they are making decisions about whether or not their office receives that much more funding. It was made clear that the worry about the incentive structure is not because police and prosecutors are bad people, but that they are having temptation thrown very subtly in their way and that it would be better for them and the public to restructure the system.

Miller spoke of several possible ways to address the problem. The first was an outright ban on civil asset forfeiture. States such as North Carolina and Minnesota have either removed the practice or limited it enough to make it obsolete. This would be a more difficult option, with opposition from several lobbies. But short of that, there are several options. A requirement that the funds not go directly to law enforcement or prosecutors' offices is a step in the right direction, removing the incentive that they have to increase the seizures. Another change that is needed urgently is to ensure that there is due process to the citizens being threatened under this practice. The burden of proof needs to be on the state instead of the citizen, giving those who have no representation a fighting chance at recovering their property. A third option is to have better reporting by the benefiting office about where the funds are coming from, what form they are being obtained in, and information about what happens in hearings, for example, whether or not the individual had representation.

Finally, almost all of the speakers referenced equitable sharing, an arrangement where law enforcement realizes that they are constrained by local laws, perhaps the asset in question isn't on the list of sizeable items, and they then alert and involve federal enforcement and prosecutors to the situation. These groups, operating on different guidelines, then seize the assets and provide the alerting authorities with a percentage of the profits. Matt Miller strongly recommended limiting or eliminating this practice.

Shannon Edmonds argued in favor of retaining the practice. While not disputing that there had been cases of misuse that should be cause for concern, he also believed that the funds procured by the practice were necessary for the continued operation of law enforcement. Quoting Latin, he argued, "misuse of something does not render it useless."

The speakers at the event represented the major stakeholders in the issue itself, and the majority agreement shows growing public opinion regarding civil asset forfeiture. Those in the audience embodied a growing desire in the state to put an end to the practice that exposes every citizen to threat of seizure. More and more people are advocating for strong reforms of the system, if not for complete abolishment. The introduction of due process into the process is urged, and restructuring the system to remove the perverse incentives supplied is pleaded for. Even the defenders of the system admit to its misuse. The upcoming session provides an opportunity for legislators to address the issue.

Civil Asset Forfeiture Reform in Texas: Fighting Contraband, Upholding Civil Liberties

Rep. David Simpson
Texas House of Representatives

Andrew Kloster
The Heritage Foundation

Shannon Edmonds
Texas District and County Attorneys Association

Matt Miller
Institute for Justice, Texas

Moderator **Derek Cohen**
The Texas Public Policy Foundation

The following is an adapted transcript from a symposium that took place at the Texas Capitol on December 8, 2014. It was co-sponsored by the Texas Public Policy Foundation, the Heritage Foundation and the Institute for Justice. Video of the event can be found online at rightoncrime.com

Derek Cohen: What is Civil Asset Forfeiture?

DEREK M. COHEN *is a policy analyst in the Center for Effective Justice at the Texas Public Policy Foundation and the Right on Crime campaign. Cohen graduated with a B.S. in Criminal Justice from Bowling Green State University and an M.S. in Criminal Justice from the University of Cincinnati, where he is currently completing his Ph.D. dissertation on the long-term costs and outcomes associated with correctional programming. His academic work can be found in* Policing: An International Journal of Police Strategies & Management *and the forthcoming* Encyclopedia of Theoretical Criminology *and* The Oxford Handbook on Police and Policing, *and has scholarly articles currently under review. He has presented several papers to the American Society of Criminology, the Academy of Criminal Justice Sciences, and the American Evaluation Association on the implementation and outcomes of various criminal justice policy issues. Prior to joining the Foundation, Cohen was a research associate with University of Cincinnati's Institute of Crime Science. He also taught classes in statistics, research methods, criminal procedure, and corrections.*

Civil asset forfeiture has been called, "an unfair exercise in forum shopping"; "a sustained assault on Fifth Amendment and due process"; and "policing for profit." Conversely, it's been referred to as "picking up the torch dropped by budget authorities interested in playing politics" and "an indispensable tool for combating increasingly sophisticated criminals." These contrasting descriptions have been used in the academic and popular press about civil asset forfeiture, the very phenomenon that we're here to discuss today.

Forfeiture proceedings are simple enough to understand in the abstract: First, an individual commits a crime and, during the commission of that crime, he may either use or come into the possession of an item of property, either real or intangible. The crime is discovered and, amongst other punishments, they are deprived of that property. Then, the state gains possession of that property and they are able to dispose of it in the manner best suited to the agencies that actually made that seizure.

Of course, as with most instances in legal procedure where the rubber hits the road, it isn't always that simple. The defendants may flee, leaving property unattended and having to be dealt with regardless. Remediable errors in criminal procedure may happen and that might actually cost the state its jurisdiction over a criminal enterprise. Police and prosecutors are then left with property— maybe even contraband—and, then, have to dispose of it regardless. In such cases, the property itself is what becomes the target of the procedural action, rather than the human perpetrator.

These proceedings are colloquially deemed *civil asset forfeiture*. It is the process of the state taking ownership of property without an attending criminal conviction. It is the legal provision that empowers this that, to some critics, creates the perverse incentive structure that some have deemed simply "for profit." One in which prosecutorial and police discretionary decisions are made more in line with what might materially come out than in the true application of justice. But again with that, is it ever that simple?

The first instance of property forfeiture, if we look back through the history of law, is when property was forfeited back in Roman law under the concept of *noxal surrender*. The concept of noxal surrender is where an item of individual property has harmed the property of another. This was, sadly to say, mostly to deal with offenses committed by slaves and then that "property," or perhaps other property, was actually used as remuneration.

This evolved in the 11th Century to the English law concept of *deodands*. Deodands are an instrument that is forfeited unto God, though in practice forfeited to the king, because of its intrinsic evil—that is, its intrinsic complicity in an evil act. To wit, people don't kill people, demonic swords kill people—and, then, those demonic swords are then rendered unto the king.

Contrast this with the *attainder forfeitures*, which were the historical analogues of criminal forfeiture. In the case of attainder forfeitures, a felon's property, both real and personal, was divvied up between their direct lord and their king as punishment for its crimes and remuneration for violation of the king's peace. This unilateral seizure of property became less prevalent in the wake of the Enlightenment and the social, cultural, and legal changes that that brought about. Robust protections emerged in common law that were also codified in the statute. Like most provisions found in the Bill of Rights, guarantee of due process and takings protections was a reaction directly responsible to crown abuses.

Protections aside, the Framers of the U.S. Constitution did not expressly outlaw forfeiture proceedings. Perhaps rightly so: in a fledgling country deep in debt both internally and externally and with a relatively small, diffused tax base, fees, tariffs, and property seizures from smugglers seeking to avoid these duties underwrote a vast majority of the U.S. government's expenses. The wholesale adoption of *in rem*—that is, "against the property"—forfeiture processes were pivotal in keeping our young country from collapse early on and, at worst, aggrieved foreign nationals seeking to circumvent U.S. law.

Now let's fast forward to today. Forfeiture on behalf of the government is practically ubiquitous at every level. Nationally, the use of equitable sharing groups that split up forfeited property has increased at a rate outpacing inflation since it was codified. This is despite the longstanding drop in crime rates.

In fiscal year 2012 alone, regional and local law enforcement entities in Texas reported closing the year with over $143 million in their forfeiture accounts. This is not part of any sort of budgeting process. To be clear, this number also includes forfeitures made pursuant to a criminal conviction. However, to actually cover the difference between the two under current law is nearly impossible. To quote Don Willett, Justice of the Texas Supreme Court in his biting dissent in *El-Ali v. Texas* (this was the adjunct case to state of Texas versus one 2004 Chevy Silverado), to quote, "the prevalent procedures of profitability compel us to reexamine the constitutional protections due to innocent property owners." This practice is what we actually chronicle in our report, *Taking Contraband Without Taking Our Liberties: Civil Asset Forfeiture Reform in Texas.*

To discuss this tricky topic, we've assembled a panel of top echelon stakeholders, from law enforcement to legal theorists and even a state representative to discuss the lay of the land and the reforms that we have coming in the 84th legislature.

Andrew Kloster: Victims–Law Enforcement's Impetus to Change

ANDREW KLOSTER *is the legal fellow in the Edwin Meese III Center for Legal and Judicial Studies at the Heritage Foundation. He focuses on civil rights, the role of the federal courts and other constitutional issues. Before joining Heritage in 2013, he was the Justice Robert H. Jackson legal fellow at the Philadelphia Foundation for Individual Rights In Education (FIRE). While at FIRE, he defended first amendment due process rights for college students and professors. Mr. Kloster has also worked on Capitol Hill and with a human rights organization under the United Nations.*

It's a little tough to be the first analyst on a panel on civil asset forfeiture because the main law is just ridiculous. Oftentimes, lawmakers will intentionally or unintentionally make the government do things that are bureaucratic and opaque. Civil asset forfeiture is a good case in point.

Forfeiture was designed to seize contraband, drug paraphernalia, or giant wads of cash that were sitting on top of a bag of drugs that the police happened upon. Nobody's going to claim the property, so it's not going to be a criminal prosecution, but the property is still out there and the police want to seize it. Or maybe it's a house that was purchased with drug money, or a house that drug deals take place in on a routine basis. All of this makes some sense. It was these core types of cases that were the impetus behind forfeiture being ramped up in the 1980s. These are the cases that my former boss, Ed Meese, talks about is when he was the 75th Attorney General of the United States. He says, "Gosh, this is why we're told we need to improve civil asset forfeiture." But nowadays we have numerous examples of police using civil asset forfeiture—not to go after these types of issues or cases, but as a revenue raiser.

I'll simply point you to three resources that you can take a look at if you want a really popular thirty-thousand foot view of these issues. First is the *New Yorker* article, "Taken" by Sarah Stillman. I think it was a watershed in terms of shedding light on this issue. Stillman gave the example of a case—an ACLU case in Tenaha, Texas, eight miles from the Louisiana border—where local police pulled over the Henderson family for driving in the left land without passing for some period of time. There are disputes about whether that was the case, but they pulled them over and said, "you know, you're driving in the passing lane.... Do you have any cash?" They did. Then the police threatened to call Louisiana's Department of Children and Family Services to take the couple's children, who were driving with them, unless they willingly signed over the cash. And this way, the police took six thousand dollars in cash from this family.

The second resource I'll point to is the series of articles in the *Washington Post* that began earlier this year which highlight numerous asset forfeiture stories. One of these stories is about Institute for Justice client Terry Dehko in Michigan and his small business. He was a grocer, and an immigrant to the

United States. His insurance company told him they would not cover any cash losses over ten thousand dollars. Okay, that's reasonable; that's insurance. So what does he do? Like any normal person would do with an insurance policy, he thinks, "If I ever get nine thousand nine hundred and ninety-nine dollars in cash, I'm going to deposit it to the bank, as I won't be able to have my insurance cover those losses." So he does this time and time again. The next thing he knows, the IRS has seized thirty-five thousand dollars in his operating account, alleging he was evading their reporting department. Because the IRS has a rule: if you make a ten thousand dollar cash deposit, you must report it to the IRS. And if you do it in a way that looks like you're evading these requirements, it's something called "structuring," which is a federal offense. So the IRS seized his cash. He ended up getting the money back thanks to pro bono representation—but when you have all of your money seized, you are really inconvenienced.

So why is it potentially a good thing for law enforcement to have forfeiture reform? First, ordinary budget appropriations are the carrot. Ordinary budget funding for law enforcement is incredibly important, and requiring local police forces to hunt for their own funding is difficult and problematic. And, while there are usually prohibitions on using forfeiture funds for personnel, there is still incredible pressure on them. It's essential to accurately fund law enforcement so they don't need to use civil forfeiture to keep their departments going.

On the other hand, the stick that's used to pressure law enforcement to support forfeiture reform is bad publicity. And, in Texas, there are a lot of victims' stories to tell.

Here's an example of a common story: a kid graduates from college somewhere on the east cost. His dad gives him cash. He wants to move to California, so he drives across country. Then, he gets stopped somewhere in Oklahoma or Texas and, for one violation or another, law enforcement ends up seizing his cash. That type of situation happens all the time. It should not be difficult for you to find examples of forfeiture abuse in or around your communities.

This issue is going to come up in the next Congressional session, because asset forfeiture reform is a bipartisan issue. As a representative of a conservative organization, I'm often united with with folks on the left and in libertarian organizations. And things are moving. Let me just mention federal reform briefly, as it will come up during 2015. Senator Rand Paul introduced a bill to remove equitable sharing, effective entirely. This contrasts to the proposals of some members of the House, who had bills that settled with merely some procedural reform.

This issue is in the popular culture now, and there are excellent resources for you to learn more about it.

Matt Miller: Due Process and Skewed Incentives

MATT MILLER *is the managing attorney at the Institute for Justice's Texas office, where he fights to secure property rights, economic relief, freedom of speech, and school choice. He represents individuals and small business owners in federal and state courts in Texas and in and around the country, including successfully defending the author and publisher of a book about eminent domain abuse after he was sued for defamation by a powerful developer. And Mr. Miller successfully litigated against the city of El Paso, Texas, to force the city to repeal a law that prohibited street vendors from operating near brick and mortar restaurants. He has also litigated on legislative repeal of a law requiring computer repair technicians to obtain a private investigator's license.*

Here are three themes that I want you to take away from this policy primer: forfeiture is big; it's a problem; and there's something that you can do about it.

Forfeiture is big in Texas. The numbers are large, in the hundreds of millions of dollars. It's big all around the country. But let's talk about why forfeiture is a problem. It's a problem both for property owners and for, I think, law enforcement officers.

But let's talk first about property owners. You've all heard the horror stories—and they're real. There are true and shocking horror stories about forfeiture from Texas and all around the country. But as important as the horror stories are, the everyday machinations of forfeiture are what I want to drill down on a little bit. And let me paint a picture for you:

Back in 2010, my colleague Scott Bullock and I were in the courtroom in Harris County, Texas. And in Harris County, one poor judge is assigned to a forfeiture docket for some period of time. So that judge, a couple of days a week, gets to hear nothing but forfeiture cases. And in this courtroom, the prosecutor is camped out and has a quasi-law office on one side of the courtroom. There are boxes of forfeiture cases. And the prosecutor and her assistants are camped out there; they'll be bringing case after case after case in front of the judge as he or she hears the forfeiture docket. There's no one on the other side of the courtroom representing property owners. And when you hear these cases being called, these are not drug kingpins. These are *State of Texas v. $823* or *State of Texas v. one 1989 Ford or Dodge Caravan.* In Minnesota, the average civil forfeiture was twelve hundred dollars. The reason there was no one on the other side of the courtroom is, it's not worth the time and expense to go to court to try to get that property back. You're not going to pay an attorney three thousand dollars to get twelve hundred dollars worth of property back. So yes, civil forfeiture is a useful tool for fighting drug kingpins and major criminals—but, more and more, it's used to take small amounts of property from ordinary Americans.

I don't know if anyone's gotten a speeding ticket lately, but you'll notice that police often ask if you have any cash on you when they pull you over. The reason they ask is that they're looking to seize and forfeit that money. Obviously, speeding has nothing to do with how much cash you may or may not have with you in the car. But you're required to answer the question truthfully. Often, local law enforcement will then seize that cash. That's why you get *State of Texas v. $832* and these relatively small amounts of money.

And so the judge will call the case. The prosecutor stands up to represent the state, and then the judge asks, "Is the property owner here?" And time after time, the property owner is not there. "Is his attorney here?" No, his attorney is not there. So the judge enters a default judgment against the property owner. You can see this in Harris County, and I'm sure it's the same in courtrooms around the state. It's a relatively petty problem, but it affects lots and lots of Texas property owners. A thousand dollars, an old Dodge Caravan, these are real assets and real property for these people. And it materially affects their lives when they're taken. They need these vehicles to drive their children to school. They need this money to buy groceries.

Forfeiture gives police an incentive to take assets without charging anyone with a crime. And that's an important point. We can have *civil* asset forfeiture reform while still leaving *criminal* asset forfeiture available as tool for law enforcement. If you bring charges that convict someone of a crime, you can take the fruits of that crime. Criminal forfeiture will still exist. But under civil forfeiture, you can take a property—never charge someone with a crime—and the burden is on the owner to get that property back.

So let's talk about why this might be a burden for law enforcement. Whenever we tell people about civil forfeiture, one way in which people will push back is they will say, "that's not actually going to skew law enforcement priorities because police are good people." And police are good people. This isn't about police or prosecutors being bad people; it's about incentives that cause good people to prioritize certain things like civil forfeiture, instead of other things, like other law enforcement activities.

We worked with some professors who conducted a study in a Nobel Prize-winning area called experimental economics. It involves a series of games that people play to test different incentive structures within those games. We wanted to see if incentives affect the behavior of ordinary people. And we found that they do. The kinds of forfeiture incentives we have in Texas and around the country actually do influence peoples' behaviors. The authors of the study concluded that the experiment's results suggest that the problem with civil forfeiture is not one of a few bad apples, but bad law that encourages bad behavior.

In other words, it is not the players; it is the game. Civil forfeiture makes individuals choose between benefiting himself or herself or the general public. And unsurprisingly, people choose to benefit themselves.

If we reform the system, we could allow police to put their effort into pursuing law enforcement goals that we can all agree on, rather than pursuing civil forfeiture. And I imagine the burden on them would be much less. Because, again, these aren't bad people. But if they have to fund thirty percent of their budget through civil forfeiture, they're going to fill the gap that way. In addition, it takes time and police energy away from other activities that can be better spent protecting the public.

So I hope you're convinced now that forfeiture is a problem, both for property owners and for police and prosecutors. Let's talk about what we can do here in Texas to address the problem. I've already suggested eliminating civil forfeiture, as they've done in North Carolina. Police and prosecutors are able to operate in that state without it. Minnesota just passed a law requiring a conviction for forfeiture. Texas could do the same thing.

But short of that, there are four things:

First, you could eliminate policing for profit by requiring police and prosecutors to take seized money and put it into some kind of general fund, rather than into a law enforcement fund. The money goes into the general fund and then the individually elected representatives decide how that money is going to be spent. A legislator, city council or county commissioner would then decide how that money gets allocated.

Second, you could provide greater protection for innocent owners. And in the forfeiture context, *innocent owner* is a technical term. I would argue that a lot of people who get their money or cars taken that aren't charged with a crime are innocent. The fact that they're not charged with a crime I think we can presume they're innocent.

But there are other, more complicated scenarios. For example, someone loans his car to his son. The son is busted for dealing drugs out of that car, and is convicted. Then, while police and prosecutors take the car, it is the actual owner's burden to prove that he didn't know the car was being used in conjunction with illegal activity. That is backwards; it should be the government's burden to show that the owner knew, or should have known, the car was being used in conjunction with illegal activity. It's very hard to prove a negative, and it's also expensive. Innocent owners who have had their cars or houses taken have to pay for their own lawyers. And then they have the burden of showing they're innocent. That's a due process problem, and we can address it by shifting the burden through a change in the law.

Third, I think we need better reporting. While we have reporting on civil asset forfeiture in Texas, we don't know enough about how it's being used on the ground. Forfeiture is an awesome power: it's the power to take someone's property—then make him or her struggle to get it back. If we're going to allow police and prosecutors to use this power, we need to know how it's being used in every case. So, let the public know exactly what is being taken. Let the public know exactly how many default judgments there are. Let the public know know whether or not the property owner hired an attorney. Let the public know where the money is going and how it is being used. This wouldn't be that hard to report. If you're going to give law enforcement this power, it should be held accountable through increased and enhanced reporting.

And finally, there is a problem with equitable sharing. No matter how Texas reforms our state laws, local law enforcement can circumvent those laws by teaming up with the federal government to split civil forfeiture money. Under this scheme, eighty percent goes to local law enforcement and twenty percent goes to the federal government. Texas can limit or eliminate equitable sharing, but I would propose a floor for equitable sharing. Some US Attorney's offices have this; they won't do equitable sharing cases where the assets are below twenty-five thousand dollars, or below fifty thousand dollars. They can still use equitable sharing for the drug kingpins in the big cases, but it eliminates the smaller, penny ante stuff. Like the stuff that I saw back in the courtroom in Harris County. This would allow Texas reforms to have some bite.

Texas values our independence from the federal government, and we should do what we can to be committed to that independence. Reforming civil asset forfeiture will go a long way towards protecting the property owners of this state.

Shannon Edmonds: Misused Doesn't Mean Useless

SHANNON EDMONDS *is the director of governmental relations at the Texas District and County Attorneys Association (TDCAA), the largest statewide association of prosecutors in the nation. Mr. Edmonds served as a liaison between prosecutors and the Texas legislature on issues of criminal justice, juvenile justice, and governmental representation issues. He also provides training, education, and assistance to members of TDCAA and other legal and law enforcement entities. Mr. Edmonds has written many articles and given presentations on the legislative process and other varieties of legal topics including capital punishment, prosecutorial ethics, DUI law, child abuse, gambling, and mental health issues.*

There is another side of civil asset forfeiture. And we can get to it by thinking about the Fence Rule—something that GK Chesterton, a great thinker, came up with. He said, "Before you take down a fence, you need to sit down and figure out why it was put up. And then, if you can figure out that that need is no longer there, take down the fence."

So, why was civil asset forfeiture created? It was created in Texas in 1989. If you know your history, you know that 1989 was close to or the peak of high crime in Texas. Compared to today, the crime rate was a hundred and twenty percent higher. We've cut crime by more than half in the last twenty-five years.

Civil asset forfeiture was created because people would get criminally convicted of crimes and then law enforcement would have to give their property back to them. Most Texans, I think, found this ridiculous. There was no mechanism for keeping criminals from enjoying the fruits of their ill-gotten labor. We all know that crime shouldn't pay; we learned that in elementary school. And civil asset forfeiture is about making sure that crime doesn't pay.

So there are two aspects of civil asset forfeiture, whether it is used or misused. But it is taking proceeds and assets away from the bad guys. And I submit that civil asset forfeiture has been very, very successful in that regard over the course of its lifetime. So why are we reevaluating it now? Well, as I say, crime rate is at a forty year low. We have ten million more people in Texas than we did in 1984, but we have the same number of crimes. Think about that: ten million more people and the same number of crimes. That means crime is not important to voters anymore. According to polls, about 3 percent of Texas voters believe crime and drugs are the state's most important issues. Immigration, border security, the economy, jobs, health care—all those things rank above criminal justice in voters' minds. If you go back twenty years to 1994, fifty-two percent of voters said crime and drugs was the most important issue. That shows how things have changed in the mentality of what's important to voters and what's important to legislators.

The second thing that has generated some movement in this is the rise of libertarianism on the right, which has been a sea change. It used to be a pretty easy dichotomy: on the left was the 'hug-a-thug' crowd; on the right, you had 'tough on crime,' or 'lock 'em up and throw away the key.' And now, you have a blending of the two in the libertarian movement. One of the things that accompany this philosophy is the proposition that, not only should the government do a few things and do them well but, in some cases, government should stop doing things altogether. "Stop taking my money." "We need to shrink government."

What is Grover Norquist's famous saying? "I don't want to abolish the government, I just want to make it small enough I can drown it in the bathtub." It's tongue-in-cheek, but it nevertheless describes a mentality that considers any revenue generated by the government as bad. Another factor contributing to the rise in debate about asset forfeiture is a general distrust of and desire to limit what our government does.

And then the third thing, of course, is always money. Money always drives the train at the Texas Capitol, and also in your local commissioner's courts. I get tickled when I hear folks say, "Well, just give up asset forfeiture and then come to the Capitol and ask for that money." Because there isn't a single Republican in the next legislature who won the primary announcing he was going to spend more money. They came to cut budgets, not increase them. So it's disingenuous to say that local law enforcement should depend on the legislature for all their funds. Remember, prosecutors and law enforcement get almost no funding from the state government.

Because there is reporting, we know that there is about a hundred and forty-two million dollars held by all the local law enforcement and prosecutors in this state. That split is usually about seventy or eighty percent law enforcement, and twenty or thirty percent for prosecutors. I just looked up the budget of the Harris County Sheriff's Office; their annual budget is three hundred and ninety-two million dollars. So all the law enforcement agencies in this entire state have less in their asset forfeiture funds than one sheriff's office. It's all relative.

But it is a problem when people abuse the system. The forfeiture statute was created in 1989 and has been amended every session since then. Every session since 1989, that chapter has been touched. And in most cases, it's been expanded.

Recently, we've seen some attempts to limit it as well. Those attempts have been inspired by some of the horror stories that you've heard. And I give credit to Senator John Whitmire in the Senate. This has been an issue that has been very interesting to him; he's taken the lead in making sure that some of those abuses are limited. And so when you hear things about police departments seizing expensive margarita machines—I mean, they made fun of that in the really funny John Oliver video on asset forfeiture—it's been ten or eleven years ago. And the District Attorney responsible lost his election, finishing third in a three-person race because of it. In Dallas we had a DA who was the darling of the media. He, too, just lost his election in part because there were questions about how he was using his asset forfeiture money. And that's how it should be. The answer is at the ballot box.

We also know that some of the reforms and oversight that have been put into place over the past ten years by Senator Whitmire and others are working. The process is working in Dallas. Prosecutors have worked with Senator Whitmire and others in the capitol to make sure that asset forfeiture is used properly.

What we're not seeing any of, however, is what good comes out of civil asset forfeiture—because government working properly is not news. It's not. It doesn't make for good quotes, it doesn't make for funny John Oliver skits or something on The Daily Show. It's boring. And frankly, I'd be happy if asset forfeiture became nice and boring.

Derek started off with quoting Roman law. I'm going to quote St. Thomas Aquinas: "Misuse of something does not render it useless." In other words, just because somebody abuses something doesn't mean it's bad. It just means that you need to address the abuses of it. And that's something that Texas has done very well lately. There's always two ways to see things.

Matt started talking about this court system, the civil court where the Harris County DA's office is hearing all of these cases. What I think is, "Man, that's a lot of due process we're doing for only eight hundred dollars." The prosecutors have to file a claim on an asset within thirty days or they have to give it up. They have to give notice to the asset's owners or, if it's a vehicle, they have to track down whose name is on it and make sure that they know that their vehicle was used in a crime or was among the proceeds of crime. They have to try to get them to court. All those things are exactly what I think most people want to happen, but you don't hear that it's happening, because that doesn't fit the narrative of advocate reform.

Rep. David Simpson: Forfeiture in a Constitutional Context

REPRESENTATIVE DAVID SIMPSON *is the state representative for Texas House of Representatives District Seven, comprised of Gregg and Upshurshire Counties. Since his first day of election in 2010, Rep. Simpson has served on the County Affairs Land and Resource Management and Joint Coastal Barrier System committees. Prior to his service in District Seven, Rep. Simpson served several terms as the mayor of Avinger, Texas. In the private sector, he is the president and chief executive officer of Avinger Timber, LLC. He has a bachelors degree in philosophy from Vanderbilt University and is a graduate of the Trinity Ministerial Academy.*

Like many government ideas gone awry, the thought behind civil asset forfeitures may have had a kernel of sense in it when it was first conceived.

The force of government should only be employed when one individual harms a neighbor. Then, it is right that government requires the use of force to compel restitution to the neighbor or to the public. And such restitution should include ill-gotten gains. Furthermore, it may be prudent for civil authorities to preclude the use of some property connected with criminal activity until conviction and sentencing has occurred. So there may be indeed a place for temporary or permanent forfeiture of property in the pursuit of justice.

While our Constitution never contemplates injustice as a means to achieve justice, civil forfeiture in the laws has been codified and enforced unjustly. Knowing that the propensity of government is to overstep its bounds, the Bill of Rights was added to the Constitution to ensure its ratification and to prevent abuse of the powers that were granted. The Fourth Amendment provides that, "the right of the people to be secure in their persons, houses, papers, and effects against unreasonable searches and seizures shall not be violated." It also provides that, "no warrant shall issue except upon probable cause afforded by oath or affirmation and particularly describing the place to be searched and the persons or things to be seized." The Fifth Amendment provides, among other things that, "no person shall be compelled in any criminal case to be a witness against himself nor deprived of life, liberty or property without due process of law. Nor shall private property be taken for public use without just compensation." Even a cursory reading of those provisions would inform an individual that the concept of forfeiture of assets should, at a minimum, require a warrant and due process before the government can take an individual's property. But that isn't what is happening.

By now many have heard about instances like those and here in Texas where police targeted minorities driving in rental vehicles for traffic stops and then confiscated large amounts of cash through coercive means. In such instances, criminal charges were not filed, and the individual was intimidated into signing over rights of property to avoid what they considered bogus charges being filed. Or, in one case, to avoid having children taken and put into foster care. That's modern day highway robbery with a twist; in this version, it's the white hat who holds up the coach and empties the pockets of the travelers, acting as judge and jury. How can they do that, you ask.

To get around those pesky little constitutional issues, legislatures, both state and federal, have created a dual system of justice whereby the assets of an individual are named in a case as we've heard. Not the individual themselves. We have established laws in Texas and in the United States where the owner of property is presumed guilty until they can prove their own property was obtained through legitimate means. The state now has a low threshold to show that property may have been used in illegal activity. The very presence of cash can be assumed to be a result of drug activity. We should not be proud of these means that effectively nullify, mute or cripple constitutional restrictions on government power.

In some states with higher standards of forfeiture than federal requirements, local and state authorities are now working with federal officials to seize assets and share the proceeds on an eighty/twenty basis with the initiating agencies. In other words, law enforcement agencies are working in conjunction with the federal government to intentionally circumvent state law.

Allowing participation in such situations is nothing less than selling our citizens to the federal government. If we expect a society of law and order, we must craft our laws to insure justice is achieved justly. We cannot allow government to steal from citizens and then condemn the citizens for doing the same activity. The taking of assets from a citizen should not be easier than the conviction of a crime.

Reforms in the area of civil forfeiture should begin with the recognition that citizens and their property should have a presumption of innocence. The burden of proving that property was the result of ill-gotten gains should be on the government, not the accused. And it should have the same standard as a criminal case. The way it is now, the owner of the property has to prove a negative.

Also, we should check improper motives. Proceeds from seized assets should be directed to crime victims or entered into defense, rather than to fund law enforcement. Law enforcement should not fund itself; it should be funded through the budgetary process.

Government should not keep property unless there is an indictment and a conviction for serious crime. Moreover, there should be appropriate requirements of timeliness to insure this provision is not abused. Property should be returned in good condition. And law enforcement should not have immunity for damage that results in financial injury to an innocent owner.

We have a Constitution dedicated to both liberty and limited government. They stand or fall together. Liberty used irresponsibly produces more government. But a government that uses force unnecessarily or unreasonably not only reduces individual liberty, but it invites anarchy. It is not good government.

In East Texas, we have a saying: "Fences keep the honest people out." Our Constitution is a fence that we need to keep and maintain to ensure good government.

Taking Contraband Without Taking Our Liberties: Civil Asset Forfeiture Reform in Texas

Derek Cohen

Texas Public Policy Foundation

Introduction

In October of 2007, Roderick Daniels was traveling through Tenaha, Texas on US Route 59. Just outside of the city, he was pulled over for allegedly traveling 37 miles-per-hour in a 35 miles-per-hour zone. The officer then asked Mr. Daniels if he was carrying any cash. The very aim of the trip being to purchase a car, he revealed to the officer that he was carrying a substantial amount of cash; about $8,500. Little did Mr. Daniels know he was about to be become a textbook case of civil asset forfeiture abuse in Texas.

The officer promptly placed Mr. Daniels under arrest and transported him to the jail. It was here that Daniels was given an ultimatum: sign pre-notarized documents agreeing to forfeit the money and jewelry found in his car, or be charged with money laundering. Scared and far from home, Mr. Daniels complied.[1]

Ron Henderson and Jennifer Boatright had a similar experience with the Tenaha Police on US Route 59. While traveling through the area with their two children, they were pulled over and questioned as to whether they were carrying cash. They, too, were looking to purchase a used car and were carrying over $6,000. The officers began searching the car, turning up no contraband. Neither officer issued a citation for the alleged offense—driving in a left-hand turn lane—and Ms. Boatright and Mr. Henderson were told that they could either sign the same documents relinquishing all ownership interest in the cash or face money laundering charges. In addition, they were told that challenging the charge would result in them being placed in custody with their two small children being placed in foster care. The couple signed over their property rather than face the dissolution of their family.[2]

Incidents such as these, while abhorrent, are not uncommon. In Tenaha alone, it is estimated that between 2006 and 2008 the police seized $3 million worth of property from motorists. Over 150 of these seizure cases are believed to be invalid.[3] With only 923 residents and two sworn police officers,[4] these enforcement actions represent a windfall to the Tenaha and Shelby County government and have the potential to underwrite a significant portion of their budget.

Absent proper procedural safeguards, the practice of forfeiture is extremely susceptible to abuse. Unfortunately, Texas ranks amongst the worst in the nation in protecting its citizens from such abuses.[5] It is easy for officials to cast too wide a net given Texas' broad statutes that contain few restrictions on civil asset forfeiture. Moreover, Texas also permits its state and local law enforcement authorities to be compensated for cooperation with federal law enforcement agencies in seizing property, thereby compromising state sovereignty by partially surrendering the police power that is a core state constitutional function.

This report summarizes the practice of civil asset forfeiture nationally and in Texas specifically. The breadth of the practice is discussed, and avenues for reform are laid out. Abusive forfeiture practices are one of the most pernicious invasions of personal liberty perpetrated in this modern age. However, there are policies available that can blunt misuse of this power.

Forfeiture in Law Enforcement

"Forfeiture" is a mechanism by which the state obtains ownership and control of an individual's property, usually via legal convention following an alleged crime. The property is often held by the government while the case is pending.

The most well-known form of asset forfeiture used in law enforcement is criminal forfeiture. Criminal forfeiture occurs when law enforcement agents make an arrest and confiscate property that ostensibly was used in the commission of a crime or whose possession came about as the fruit of a criminal act. After a finding of guilt or guilty plea, ownership of the property is fully turned over to the state.

This property is usually liquidated through a police auction or, in the event an item could be of direct value to the police, repurposed for their use. It is not uncommon to see a high-end car seized from a drug dealer being outfitted with lights and siren and used an interceptor. This form of forfeiture is laudable. Among the benefits: 1) it forces law-breakers to subsidize law enforcement through their ill-gotten gains, and 2) the full transfer of ownership interest occurs after a guilty verdict or plea, thereby preserving the due process of the criminal court.

The practice of civil asset forfeiture operates in a more ambiguous area of law. Unlike legal action taken against a person under the allegation of criminal conduct, and all the procedural safeguards that entails, civil forfeiture targets the property itself, not the owner, and can occur regardless of whether any criminal charges are brought forth. These actions are a form of in rem proceedings, or accusations against property.

This legal fiction of sentient property has led to nonsensical case names such as United States vs. $124,700 in US Currency, *United States vs. One Pearl Necklace*, and *.39 Acres vs. the State of Texas*.

The tradition of in rem jurisdiction dates back to the medieval common law practice of deodand seizures. A deodand, strictly speaking, is "an instrument causing another person's death."[6] Kings were able to, without conviction of the property owner, seize the item in order to provide restitution to the slain person's family. The prevailing superstition of the time was that such objects could possess the requisite capacity and sentience to deliberately harm an individual and therefore could be directly "punished" by being seized.[7] The practice was relied upon heavily in the early days of the United States, specifically in the enforcement customs duties. Funding nearly the entirety of the federal government in its infancy, agents were empowered to seize property for which the proper tax had not been paid. Upheld in early Supreme Court cases, it was not until after the Civil War that civil asset forfeiture was applied outside of the maritime law.*

In a criminal case, the government must prove their case against the accused individual beyond a reasonable doubt. However, having no such implicit protections, the burden of proof to seize property during civil forfeiture proceedings is often much lower. Most states, as well as the federal government, employ a "preponderance of the evidence" standard, meaning that it is more likely than not what the seizing agency says is true as determined by a judge. A handful of states have lower standards, while others have increased procedural safeguards to the level tantamount to a criminal case.

In some forfeiture cases, seizures have been made without an allegation of criminal conduct, much less one proven before a court, and in the complete absence of any corroborating evidence. For example, the Internal Revenue Service has recently made several high-profile "structuring" seizures. Pursuant to the Currency and Foreign Transactions Reporting Act of 1970 (or the "Bank Secrecy Act"), banks are required to report all deposits of negotiable instruments in excess of $10,000 in aggregate in one day into a single account. Deposits of this size, the government alleges, can be indicative of tax evasion or money laundering and, therefore, need to be tracked. As a result, Congress has made it illegal to "structure" numerous deposits so that they fall underneath the reporting requirement. However, since Congress eliminated 'willfulness' as an element of the crime, a pattern of suspicious transactions alone is sufficient for prosecution or, as will be discussed here, to have someone's property seized. In one such case, a Michigan grocery store owners' insurance policy covered only up to $10,000 worth of cash loss, leading them to deposit the cash-on-hand upon approaching the insurance cap. Seeing this as an attempt to evade the deposit threshold, the IRS seized the grocery proprietors' bank account and emptied it of its balance that totaled over $35,000.[9] After facing substantial media scrutiny and pro bono litigation by the Institute for Justice, the IRS

---

*·For a full discussion of the evolution of civil forfeiture practices from ancient history to the present in including relevant discussion of rationale, please see Boudreaux & Pritchard's "Civil orfeiture and the War on Drugs: Lessons from Economics and History" from the *San Diego Law Review* (1996).

eventually agreed to return the money. However, this came nearly a year after the seizure with no charges ever having been filed.[10]

This has given rise to the allegation of "policing for profit," or engaging in law enforcement activities based solely on the potential payouts of forfeited property.[11] There is a good deal of evidence to support the existence of this practice. A survey reporting the responses of 770 law enforcement agencies found that nearly 40 percent viewed the proceeds of civil forfeiture as a necessary supplement to their budgets.12 This suggests that law enforcement administration may find themselves in a situation where pecuniary departmental interests overshadow their deference to substantive and procedural law. This is further substantiated by attempts to circumvent state safeguards via equitable sharing practices involving the federal government, as seen below. This is echoed by accounts of forfeited funds being spent on exotic travel and recreational items.

Another problematic aspect of civil asset forfeiture is that the legal costs associated with recovering one's property often far exceed the value of the property itself. Since the seizing agency is acting under the color of law, parties who have been victims of this abuse generally may not recover legal fees or punitive damages, such as those that can be part of the relief and remediation under a federal civil rights action brought under §1983.13 For those without deep pockets, they may not be able to afford a lawyer, and the inability to recover damages makes it difficult to find counsel willing to work on a contingency fee. Accordingly, asserting one's presumption of innocence and rights to property ownership can often be contingent on receiving pro bono support from a public interest law firm. Even for those with personal resources, when the value of the property exceeds the legal expenses, there is little incentive to incur the cost of spending time and money to recover property that is worth less than the opportunity cost involved.

There has been some passing legislative interest in limiting the use of the civil asset forfeiture. The United States Congress recognized these problems in 2000 when it passed the Civil Asset Forfeiture Reform Act, or CAFRA. Fundamentally a milquetoast set of reforms, CAFRA did manage to reestablish the "innocent owner" affirmative defense as federal policy (previously invalidated in

Bennis v. Michigan),[14] though the burden of proof both in the federal government and most states remained on the owner of the property.[15] As illustrated anecdotally above and quantitatively below, however, forfeiture practices seem to have only have become more problematic since CAFRA's passage.

Equitable Sharing: The 21st Century "Silver Platter"

Perhaps even more caustic to liberty is equitable sharing; a practice through which federal agents and unscrupulous state or local law enforcement officials can collude to sidestep state law that protects citizens from forfeiture abuse.

In 1868, the United States Congress passed the 14th Amendment to the Constitution. As the most philosophically far-reaching of the Reconstruction Amendments, the 14th Amendment guaranteed American citizens, amongst other rights, equal protection under law and reaffirmed the 5th Amendment's due process provision. The latter, in this context, has been interpreted by the courts as applying directly to state law. This has paved the way for the other individual liberty protections against government action set forth in the Constitution, namely the Bill of Rights, to be applied to state level actors as well.

This has led to some novel legal theories that capitalize on parallel federal and state criminal jurisdiction. In the time between the 4th Amendment being given "teeth" via the exclusionary rule in *Weeks v. United States* and incorporated to the states in *Mapp v. Ohio*, it was not uncommon for cooperating law enforcement agencies to circumvent procedural safeguards on evidence gathering. Unable to use the evidentiary fruits of an unconstitutional search in criminal prosecutions, federal law enforcement agencies would rely on state law enforcement—not yet bound by the exclusionary rule—to make dubious searches and supply the evidence to federal officials. This end-around was known as the "silver platter doctrine," referencing the manner in which the evidentiary material was served up to the prosecuting authorities.

The doctrine continued until 1960, when the U.S. Supreme Court's ruling in *Elkins v. United States* explicitly forbade the practice. The dissenting justices argued that suppressing the silver platter doctrine would represent an affront to the principles of federalism and deference to the several states' responsibility to establish and enforce criminal law. Of course, allowing the doctrine would wholly abdicate the procedural safeguards guaranteed to all United States citizens to the whims of state-level bureaucrats. This holding was bolstered by *Mapp* four years later, a ruling that incorporated the full array of 4th Amendment protections to the states.

A similar practice has emerged in the area of civil asset forfeiture. The practice of "equitable sharing" is a mechanism whereby property seized by federal law enforcement agencies is shared, in part or in whole, with cooperating state and local agencies. This can equate to as much as 80 percent of the total value of seized property being shared.

Ironically, equitable sharing is arguably the largest threat to the principles of federalism, individual liberty notwithstanding, since it allows federal authorities and local law enforcement agencies to circumvent state law. Accordingly, federal seizures have occurred in which no state law was being violated. For example, California medicinal marijuana dispensaries, fully in compliance with state law on the matter, have had their locations raided and property seized for being in violation of federal laws.[16] With the perverse incentives plainly apparent, local agencies can be coopted into enforcing federal statutes that the constituents of their state have not accepted, and enriching the agency doing so.

In addition, many states have attempted to implement procedural safeguards against forfeiture abuse, some even requiring the same burden of proof being placed on the government as in a criminal trial. However, through joint investigative forfeitures, state/local and federal agencies may cooperate in an investigation and seize property under the less-restrictive federal standard. This property would still be liquidated and its value shared with the state/local agency even if the state had adopted laws and procedures that protect its citizens against this practice.

There is a growing amount of quantitative support to the idea that state and local law enforcement agencies are using equitable sharing agreements to circumvent state-imposed safeguards. Using data from both the Law Enforcement Management and Administrative Statistics (LEMAS) survey as well as federal forfeiture data, a 2011 study found that local law enforcement agencies were more likely to use equitable sharing as a forfeiture mechanism if the state had procedural safeguards or a higher burden of proof.[17]

Forfeiture as a National Phenomenon

Estimates of the pervasiveness of civil asset forfeiture are difficult to come by. The bulk of forfeiture occurs at the local level, and few states have structured reporting systems where all entities from small villages to sprawling cities must report the amounts seized and liquidated. Further, those that do require reports often allow for the aggregation of the value of all forfeited property, making it impossible to delineate legitimate criminal forfeiture from civil asset forfeiture from administrative forfeiture and so on.

One method to capture the pervasiveness of forfeiture nationally is to consider responses to the LEMAS survey. The survey has been given intermittently for the past three decades, and what is being measured has changed in nearly every version. Regardless of these issues, responses can be tallied to illustrate how widespread the practice of forfeiture is at the local level.

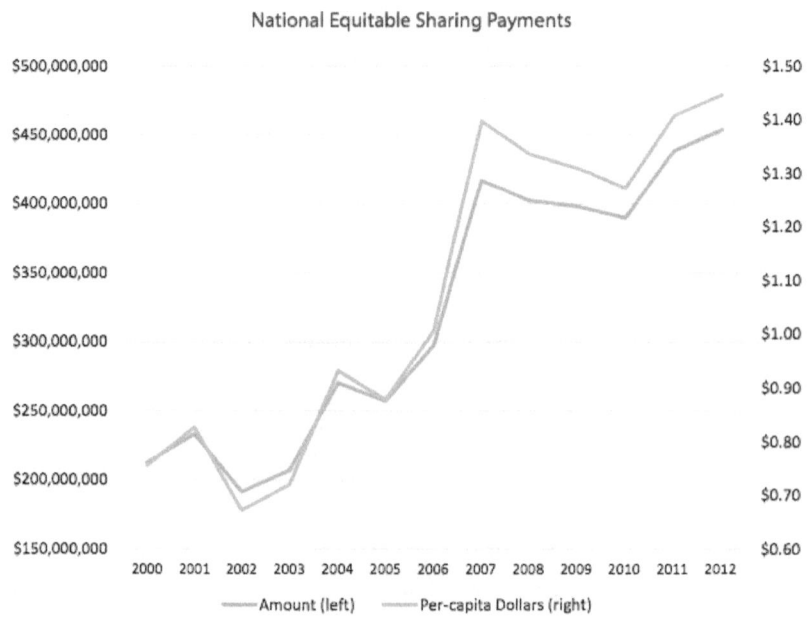

National Equitable Sharing Payments

In 2007, the last year the survey was issued, state and local law enforcement agencies nationwide indicated that they had seized an estimated total of $825,468,951 worth of assets. The primary driver behind this figure was the $718,180,370 of drug-related seizures, a figure that would span the range of actions from legitimate criminal forfeitures to pretextual civil forfeiture. The previous survey, conducted in 2003, reflected that self-reported drug-related seizures totaled $415,350,136,18 an increase of nearly 73 percent over the four year interim, while drug use across a variety of metrics—most notably in the percentage people having ever used marijuana, cocaine, crack-cocaine, heroin, or methamphetamines, the most highly-trafficked drugs—has markedly decreased over the same time period.[19] "Other forfeiture programs" contributed $101,909,366, and seizures of property relating to illegal gambling amounted to $5,379,215 in 2007.[20]

The use of equitable sharing has also grown immensely in recent years. In 2000, federal law enforcement agencies made $212,438,950 in equitable sharing payments to state and local entities. In 2012, that number has more than doubled to $453,814,470. To put this in perspective, this equates to just over 75 cents per person nationwide in 2000 and nearly $1.45 per person in 2012.21

Forfeiture in Texas

In Texas, the legal standard for civil asset forfeiture is preponderance of the evidence, meaning that the seizing agency need only convince a judge that their account of the facts of the case (and implicit criminal conduct) is more likely than not to be true.[22] Of course, this standard only applies if the aggrieved party attempts to assert their ownership interests. Otherwise, the forfeiture proceeds uncontested.

In *Policing for Profit*, a 2010 nationwide report by the Institute for Justice, Texas was given an overall grade of "D-," which includes a "D" for existing forfeiture protections and the amount of proceeds that directly benefit Texas law enforcement and an "F" for the state's overreliance on equitable sharing.23

How Much is Going On?

The prevalence of forfeiture in the State of Texas has followed the national trend. Both the sum value and per-capita dollars of seized property have risen rapidly while triggering events, as measured in both official and self-report data, have been plummeting. Of the $825 million reported above, $49 million were seizures reported by the 200 responding Texas agencies.[24]

Equitable sharing payments have followed suit. In 2001, Texas received $19,668,285 from the federal government compared to $31,520,522 in 2012. This trend holds even in light of Texas' skyrocketing population, growing from 92 cents to $1.21 per person for the same years, respectively. From 2000 through 2006, Texas received an average of 88 cents each year per capita, while this increased to almost $1.29 per person the period between 2007 and 2012, showing persistence even in the volatile data.[25]

What are Proceeds Being Spent On?

Data on local-level expenditures are unavailable. While the Attorney General's Office mandates that all law enforcement entities fill out a reporting form, this only pertains to items seized under Chapter 59 of the Code of Criminal Procedure.[26] As previously discussed, this would be limited to any items or contraband seized and/or liquidated under criminal forfeiture laws and would ignore property seized under civil asset forfeiture proceedings. In addition, while the reporting form does ask about potentially frivolous expenditures like travel and "buy money," it would not account for whether the money spent on these items were truly pursuant to legitimate law enforcement objectives.

However, data on state-level expenditures for over the past five years (2008–2013) for Texas are available. Upon request the Legislative Budget Board (LBB)—Texas' legislature-affiliated research and evaluation body—has provided an enumerated list of Department of Public Safety's (DPS) expenditures made with the assets held in the forfeiture fund. Granted, this is but one agency and not locally-based, but items on the expenditure report are not wholly dissimilar to what local agencies spend forfeiture money on: $300 thousand on aerial surveillance equipment; $585 thousand on in-car video equipment (with another $1 million on replacement); $12.25 million over the five-year span on aircraft—each a legitimate law enforcement tool. Other expenditures, such as $230 thousand on "covert surveillance equipment, a quarter-million dollars spent on a "Bearcat" armored vehicle, and almost $300 thousand on cellular phone tracking equipment could have legitimate law enforcement uses.[27]

However, there is a troubling trend apparent in the data. The $9.6 million DPS has paid in expenditures for the recruiting class of Fiscal Year 2011 and 2013 represents planned, operational expenses that should have been provided for by general appropriations.[28] Paying for such items through a non-recurring source like the forfeiture fund has the potential to corrupt forfeiture practices, as alluded to in the "policing for profit" literature.[29] Decisions to engage in law enforcement-related activities such as stops and asset seizures should be determined exclusively by factors legally relevant to the situation, free from the conflict-of-interest brought that having to seize property just to keep the patrol cars fueled inherently causes.

Civil Forfeiture Reform in Texas: Promising Solutions

Texas has the opportunity to implement pointed, simple procedural reforms that will both stop abusive forfeiture practices, allow the government to still claim property used in or garnered from criminal activity, and redeploy the property or apply its value for legitimate activities.

Reverting the Burden of Proof to the State

Through small procedural amendments to Chapter 59 of the Code of Criminal Procedure, Texas can establish that its law enforcement agencies must prove their case before any transfer of ownership occurs, outside of default judgement, rather than the property owner having to establish their innocence. This would not fully address the level of the burden of proof, but it would wholly restore the automatic presumption of innocence. This would also obviate the need for an "innocent owner" provision.

Even while shifting the burden of proof in civil asset forfeiture to the state, the state could still be allowed to seize property in certain circumstances before a person has been convicted. Under this approach, the state could seize property for a limited period before criminal charges are filed, such as 72 hours if there is an allegation of serious felony. Moreover, the state could only keep the property after 72 hours if it has obtained a court ruling that finds that there is a high likelihood of both conviction and the property being ultimately unrecoverable if it is returned pending the resolution of the case. While this approach would still allow for civil asset forfeiture in some cases, even in these cases the burden would be on the government to go to court to keep the property beyond 72 hours, which is far different from the current regime where the burden is on the individual to initiate action seeking return of their property.

Elevating the Standard of Sufficiency to Trigger Forfeiture

Texas could also elevate the standard to satisfy the burden of proof in forfeiture proceedings. Following the lead of other states with stronger forfeiture protections, legislation could be introduced that requires the state to prove its case beyond a reasonable doubt, akin to criminal proceedings. At least, clear and convincing evidence should be required, not merely the current preponderance of the evidence standard, which is merely a 51 percent or "slightly more likely than not" bar to clear.

Abolish the Practice Entirely

Perhaps the simplest way to ensure that civil asset forfeiture abuse is curtailed would be to outlaw the practice entirely. This would require law enforcement agencies to prove their case to a criminal court before keeping and liquidating seized property.[30] Once a guilty plea or guilty finding is entered, the agency can dispose of the property as they wish. This would ensure sanctity of the practice and also preserve the accused's due process guarantees.

North Carolina has no effective civil forfeiture provision provided by law. State and local agencies must prove their case to criminal standards if they are to keep seized property. While this is certainly laudable, it comes as no surprise that North Carolina agencies draw copious amounts from the federal equitable sharing fund. There is some consolation to be found in the increased reporting needed by the federal government to remand the funds to the states. North Carolina's example illustrates the need for additional reform, such as implementing the two reforms discussed immediately below, to curtail equitable sharing abuse if Texas were to abolish the practice of civil asset forfeiture.

Require the Attorney General to Approve Equitable Sharing Payments

While Texas can do little to curb the abuse of the equitable sharing pass-through, it can demand a higher standard of its law enforcement agencies. The Legislature can mandate that if local agencies are to participate in an equitable sharing agreement with the federal authorities, any funds seized from alleged activities not in violation of state law must be approved by the Attorney General. This will allow statewide elected oversight and suppress abusive practices by local authorities.

Further, the Legislature can mandate that no agency may engage in equitable sharing agreements until the procedural safeguards mentioned above are implemented.

Establish a Common Pool for Holding Forfeiture Funds

Texas can provide further disincentives to the practice by establishing a general fund through which the proceeds of seized assets are deposited. From this fund, agencies would receive a share based on a formula that accounts for department size, population policed, proximity to the national border, and other relevant inputs. While this would not wholly preclude forfeiture abuse, this would lay to rest the allegations of directly "policing for profit."

The Limits of Reporting Mandates and Restrictions on Expenditures

A precise accounting for what the proceeds of seizures have purchased is very difficult to obtain, even in jurisdictions that do report the activities of a forfeiture fund. Given the fungible nature of cash and the value of liquidated assets, nearly any expenditure made by an agency after having seized property or receiving equitable sharing payments could be the result of not having to spend the equivalent value elsewhere in their budget.

For example, suppose an agency seizes $50,000 worth of assets and, as an unrelated coincidence, wishes to refurbish their break room with nice furniture, electronics, and beverage machines. The agency could apply $50,000 of the forfeiture fund to salaries, equipment repair, or the like, while covering the renovations with general expenditures.

For this reason, it is unlikely that restricting what forfeiture funds may be spent on will have any discernable effect, as general funds may be spent in lieu and later substituted. Even if legislation were passed saying forfeiture proceeds could only be spent on bullet-proof protective gear and squad cars, the money originally appropriated for these items could be spend on the frivolities mentioned above.

Transparency provisions or mandatory reporting requirements of forfeiture takings, revenues, and expenditures, such as those enacted in Texas in 2011, can contribute to an overall increase in perceived trust and legitimacy, but only insofar as it accurately reflects the use of the practice.31 Even under the assumption of 100 percent compliance and accuracy, sunlight may provide little incentive to discontinue a practice that nets such benefits.

Conclusion

Texas and federal law fail to provide sufficient protections given the grave impact forfeiture typically has on affected individuals and businesses. Few legitimate legal scholars find fault with depriving criminals of the fruits of their illicit activities, but even fewer support establishing a framework wherein the innocent must underwrite a costly affirmative defense of their ownership interests. Such a system is anathema to the founding principles of this nation and, more plainly, the State of Texas.

While Texas' per-capita equitable sharing receipts are not significantly different than the national average, this does not mitigate the perversity of the practice. Just as our mothers all told us as children, "Just because everyone else is doing something doesn't mean that it's OK for you to do it, too."

Commonsense reforms in this area are easily attainable through simple procedural adjustments. By shifting the burden of proof to the state, law enforcement agencies will be required to successfully argue their claim to the property (i.e., that the property was party to or fruit of criminal activity) before the forfeiture is considered valid. By elevating the sufficiency standard to "clear and convincing evidence" or even "beyond a reasonable doubt," state officials will have a higher benchmark to clear in order to keep an individual's property. Texas can lead the way in implementing these state-level reforms.

Texas cannot do much unilaterally to stem the cooptation of state and local law enforcement through equitable sharing abuse. However, this is an opportunity for Texas to take a stand on the matter. Even if the federal government keeps abusing its power and diminishing the rule of law, Texas can refuse to be part of the practice. It can forcefully say, "I stand up for my residents' liberty"—a point the federal government has not been able to claim for some time.

Ensuring the proceeds of forfeitures are returned to the general fund and then appropriated for those legitimate law enforcement and prosecution expenses would also yield greater transparency and honesty in the budget process. Over the long term, it could also benefit the agencies involved by ensuring that, in a year when asset forfeitures fall short, those funds can be supplemented with general revenue so they are not left unable to perform their vital duties to the public.

The current practice of civil asset forfeiture, even when used prudently, erodes the Fifth Amendment's guarantee of due process and prohibition against unlawful takings, because of the limited and after-the-fact recourse available to affected individuals and businesses. The concentrated financial benefits to the government are clear, but can one truly measure the diffused cost of the erosion of liberty, rule of law, and legitimacy of government?

The white paper, "Civil Asset Forfeiture Reform in Texas" is available online at:
http://www.texaspolicy.com/sites/default/files/documents/2014-03-PP09-CivilAssetForteitureReformInTexas-CEJ-DerekCohen.pdf

Endnotes

1. Gary Tuchman & Katherine Wojtecki, "Texas Police Shake Down Drivers, Lawsuit Claims", CNN, 2009.

2. Morrow vs. City of Tenaha, et al., 2-08-cv-288-TJW (E.D. Tex.)

3. Tuchman & Wojtecki, 2009.

4. U.S. Census Bureau American Community Survey, 2011; Bureau of Justice Statistics Census of State and Local Law Enforcement Agencies (CSLLEA), 2008.

5. Marian Williams, Jefferson Holcomb, Tomislav Kovandzic, & Scott Bullock, "Policing for Profit: The Abuse of Civil Asset Forfeiture", Report from the Institute for Justice, 2010.

6. Donald Boudreaux & A.C. Pritchard, "Civil Forfeiture and the War on Drugs: Lessons from Economics and History", *San Diego Law Review*, 33 (1996) 94.

7. Ibid.

8. Williams, et. al., 2010.

9. Bob Ewing, "Taken: Federal Lawsuit in Michigan Challenges Forfeiture Abuse."

10. Bob Ewing, "IRS Backs Down: Michigan Forfeiture Case Voluntarily Dismissed."

11. Williams et al., 2010.

12. John Worrall, "Addicted to the Drug War: The Role of Civil Asset Forfeiture as a Budgetary Necessity in Contemporary Law Enforcement," *Journal of Criminal Justice*, 2001.

13. Karen Blum & Kathryn Urbanya, "Section 1983 Litigation," Federal Judicial Center, 1998.

14. *Bennis v. Michigan*, 516 U.S. 442,1996.

15. Civil Asset Forfeiture Reform Act of 2000 (HR 1658), Pub. L. No. 106-185, 106th Cong., 2000.

16. Karl Dicky, "California Property Owner Wins Forfeiture Case from Marijuana Use on Property," *The Examiner*.

17. Jefferson Holcomb, Tomislav Kovandzic, & Marian Williams, "Civil Asset Forfeiture, Equitable Sharing, and Policing for Profit in the United States," *Journal of Criminal Justice*, 2011.

18. Bureau of Justice Statistics Census of State and Local Law Enforcement Agencies (CSLLEA), 2004.

19. Substance Abuse and Mental Health Services Administration (SAMHSA), "National Survey on Drug Use and Health, 2007"; Substance Abuse and Mental Health Services Administration (SAMHSA), "National Survey on Drug Use and Health, 2003."

20. Bureau of Justice Statistics, 2008.

21. U.S. Department of Justice, Asset Forfeiture Program "Reports to Congress," years 2000-2008.

22. Scott Bullock & Dick Carpenter II, "Forfeiting Justice: How Texas Police & Prosecutors Cash In on Seized Property" Report from the Institute for Justice, 2010.

23. Williams et al., 2010 at 92.

24. Bureau of Justice Statistics, 2008.

25. U.S. Department of Justice, 2000-2012.

26. Texas Code of Criminal Procedure, "Chapter 59: Forfeiture of Contraband."

27. Texas Department of Public Safety, "Federal & State Seized Funds Summary of Revenues and Expenditures, 2008-4/2013." Personal correspondence.

28. Ibid.

29. Williams et al., 2010; Holcomb, Kovandzic, & Williams, 2011; Worrall, 2001.

30. Williams et al., 2010.

31. Texas Senate Bill 316, 2011. Texas Code of Criminal Procedure, "Chapter 59: Forfeiture of Contraband."

About Right on Crime

Right on Crime is a national campaign to promote successful, conservative solutions on American criminal justice policy—reforming the system to ensure public safety, shrink government, and save taxpayers money. By sharing research and policy ideas and mobilizing strong conservative voices, we work to raise awareness of the growing support for effective reforms within the conservative movement. We are transforming the debate on criminal justice in America.

Our Statement Of Principles

As members of the nation's conservative movement, we strongly support constitutionally limited government, transparency, individual liberty, personal responsibility, and free enterprise. We believe public safety is a core responsibility of government because the establishment of a well- functioning criminal justice system enforces order and respect for every person's right to property and life, and ensures that liberty does not lead to license.

Conservatives correctly insist that government services be evaluated on whether they produce the best possible results at the lowest possible cost, but too often this lens of accountability has not focused as much on public safety policies as other areas of government. As such, corrections spending has expanded to become the second fastest growing area of state budgets—trailing only Medicaid.

Conservatives are known for being tough on crime, but we must also be tough on criminal justice spending. That means demanding more cost-effective approaches that enhance public safety. A clear example is our reliance on prisons, which serve a critical role by incapacitating dangerous offenders and career criminals but are not the solution for every type of offender. And in some instances, they have the unintended consequence of hardening nonviolent, low-risk offenders—making them a greater risk to the public than when they entered.

Applying the following conservative principles to criminal justice policy is vital to achieving a cost-effective system that protects citizens, restores victims, and reforms wrongdoers.

1. As with any government program, the criminal justice system must be transparent and include performance measures that hold it account- able for its results in protecting the public, lowering crime rates, reducing re-offending, collecting victim restitution and conserving taxpayers' money.

2. Crime victims, along with the public and taxpayers, are among the key "consumers" of the criminal justice system; the victim's conception of justice, public safety, and the offender's risk for future criminal conduct should be pri- oritized when determining an appropriate punishment.

3. The corrections system should emphasize public safety, personal re- sponsibility, work, restitution, community service, and treatment— both in probation and parole, which supervise most offenders, and in prisons.

4. An ideal criminal justice system works to reform amenable offenders who will return to society through harnessing the power of families, charities, faith-based groups, and communities.

5. Because incentives affect human behavior, policies for both offenders and the corrections system must align incentives with our goals of public safety, victim restitution and satisfaction, and cost-effectiveness, thereby moving from a system that grows when it fails to one that rewards results.

6. Criminal law should be reserved for conduct that is either blamewor- thy or threatens public safety, not wielded to grow government and undermine economic freedom.

These principles are grounded in time-tested conservative truths— constitutionally limited government, transparency, individual liberty, personal responsibility, free enterprise, and the centrality of the family and community. All of these are critical to addressing today's criminal justice challenges. It is time to apply these principles to the task of delivering a better return on tax- payers' investments in public safety. Our security, prosperity, and freedom de- pend on it.

Right on Crime Signatories

Newt Gingrich
Former Speaker of the House of Representatives

Grover Norquist
Americans for Tax Reform

Gov. Asa Hutchinson
Governor of Arkansas

Chuck Colson (1931-2012)
Prison Fellowship Ministries

William J. Bennett
Former Secretary of Education and Federal "Drug Czar"

Jeb Bush
Former Governor of Florida

Ken Cuccinelli
Former Attorney General, Virginia

David Keene
Former Chairman, American Conservative Union and National Rifle Association

J.C. Watts
Former Member of the U.S. House of Representatives, Oklahoma's 4th District

Edwin Meese III
Former U.S. Attorney General

Stephen Moore
The Heritage Foundation

Pat Nolan
Director, Criminal Justice Reform Project, American Conservative Union Foundation

Richard Viguerie
ConservativeHQ.com

Brooke Rollins
Texas Public Policy Foundation

Ken Blackwell
Former Ohio Secretary of State

Ralph Reed
Founder, Faith and Freedom Coalition

Eli Lehrer
R Street Institute

Rebecca Hagelin
Executive Committee, Council for National Policy

Tony Perkins
Family Research Council

B. Wayne Hughes, Jr.
Businessman and Philanthropist

Henry Juszkiewicz
CEO of Gibson Guitar

Penny Nance
Concerned Women for America

John J. DiLulio, Jr.
University of Pennsylvania

Ward Connerly
American Civil Rights Institute

George Kelling
Manhattan Institute

Gary Bauer
American Values

David Barton
WallBuilders

Rabbi Daniel Lapin
American Alliance of Jews and Christians

Michael Reagan
The Reagan Legacy Foundation

Monica Crowley, Ph.D.
Fox News political analyst

Erick Erickson
Founder of RedState.com

Alfred Regnery
Law Enforcement Legal Defense Fund

Viet Dinh
Georgetown University Law Center, former U.S. Assistant Attorney General

Ronald F. Scheberle
American Legislative Exchange Council

Larry Thompson
Former U.S. Deputy Attorney General

Deborah Daniels
Former U.S. Attorney and Assistant U.S.
Attorney General

Donald Devine
Former Director, Office of Personnel
Management

Richard Doran
Former Florida Attorney General

Jim Petro
Former Ohio Attorney General

Hal Stratton
Former New Mexico Attorney General

Joe Whitley
Former Acting U.S. Associate Attorney General
and U.S. Attorney

BJ Nikkel
Former Majority Whip, Colorado House of
Representatives

Kris Steele
Former Speaker, Oklahoma House of
Representatives

Allan Bense
Former Speaker, Florida House of
Representatives

For a more complete list of Right on Crime signatories—including state-based signatories and partners—see rightoncrime.com

The Conservative Case for Criminal Justice Reform

PUBLIC SAFETY. Because government exists to secure liberties that can only be enjoyed to the extent there is public safety, state and local policymakers must make fighting crime their top priority, including utilizing prisons to incapacitate violent offenders and career criminals. Prisons are overused, however, when nonviolent offenders who may be safely supervised in the community are given lengthy sentences. Prisons provide diminishing returns when such offenders emerge more disposed to re-offend than when they entered prison.

RIGHT-SIZING GOVERNMENT. Nearly 1 in every 100 American adults is in prison or jail. When you add in those on probation or parole, almost 1 in 33 adults is under some type of control by the criminal justice system. When Ronald Reagan was president, the total correctional control rate was 1 in every 77 adults. This represents a significant expansion of government power. By reducing excessive sentence lengths and holding nonviolent offenders accountable through prison alternatives, public safety can often be achieved consistent with a legitimate, but more limited, role for government.

FISCAL DISCIPLINE. The prison system now costs states more than $50 billion per year, up from $11 billion in the mid-1980s. It has been the second-fastest growing area of state budgets, trailing only Medicaid, and consumes one in every 14 general fund dollars. Conservatives must address runaway spending on prisons just as they do with education and health care, subjecting the same level of skepticism and scrutiny to all expenditures of taxpayers' funds.

VICTIM SUPPORT. In 2008, Texas probationers paid $45 million in restitution to victims, but prisoners paid less than $500,000 in restitution, fines, and fees. Making victims whole must be prioritized when determining appropriate punishments for offenders. The criminal justice system should be structured to ensure that victims are treated with dignity and respect and that they may participate in the criminal justice process and receive restitution.

PERSONAL RESPONSIBILITY. With some 5 million offenders on probation or parole, it's critical that the corrections system hold these offenders accountable for their actions by holding a job or performing community service, attending required treatment programs, and staying crime- and drug-free. When the system has real teeth, the results can be dramatic: offenders subject to swift, certain and commensurate sanctions for rule violations in Hawaii's HOPE program are less than half as likely to be arrested or fail a drug test.

GOVERNMENT ACCOUNTABILITY. More than 40 percent of released offenders return to prison within three years of release, and in some states, recidivism rates are closer to 60 percent. As Right on Crime signatories Newt Gingrich and Mark Earley have asked, "[i]f two-thirds of public school students dropped out, or two-thirds of all bridges built collapsed within three years, would citizens tolerate it?" Corrections funding should be partly linked to outcomes and should implement proven strategies along the spectrum between basic probation and prison.

FAMILY PRESERVATION. According to National Review, "40 percent of low-income men who father a child out of wedlock have already been in jail or prison by the time their first son or daughter is born." The family unit is the foundation of society. In a society in which too many young men are incarcerated, marriage rates are depressed and far too many children grow up in single-parent homes. Instead of harming families, the corrections system must harness the power of charities, faith-based groups, and communities to reform offenders and preserve families.

FREE ENTERPRISE. The Constitution lists only three federal crimes, but the number of statutory federal crimes has now swelled to around 4,500. This is to say nothing of the thousands of bizarre state-level crimes, such as the 11 felonies in Texas related to the harvesting of oysters. The explosion of non-traditional criminal laws grows government and undermines economic freedom. Criminal law should be reserved for conduct that is blameworthy or threatens public safety, not wielded to regulate non-fraudulent economic activity involving legal products.